Leckie✕Leckie
Scotland's leading educational publishers

Practice Papers for SQA Exams

Higher

Business

Management

© 2015 Leckie & Leckie Ltd
Cover © ink-tank and associates

001/27012015

10 9 8 7 6 5 4 3 2 1

ISBN 9780007590964

Published by
Leckie & Leckie Ltd
An imprint of HarperCollins*Publishers*
Westerhill Road, Bishopbriggs, Glasgow, G64 2QT
T: 0844 576 8126   F: 0844 576 8131
leckieandleckie@harpercollins.co.uk
www.leckieandleckie.co.uk

Publisher: Katherine Wilkinson
Project managers: Craig Balfour and Sonia Dawkins

Special thanks to
Rob Jackson (author)
Lee Coutts (advisor)
Felicity Kendall (proofread)
Louise Robb (copy edit)
QBS (layout)

Dedicated to the loving memory of Jean Jackson

Printed in Italy by Lego S.P.A.

A CIP Catalogue record for this book is available from the British Library.

Acknowledgements

Marking principles p44–45 © *Scottish Qualifications Authority*

The Publishers would like to thank the following organisations for allowing reuse of their material:

p14–16 © *Merlin Entertainment plc*
p22–24 © *H&M Group*
p30–32 © *Volkswagen Group*
p32 © *European Automobile Manufacturers Association*
p38–40 © *British Airways plc*
p39 © *TM Corporate Group*

Introduction

This book contains practice exam papers that mirror the actual SQA exam as much as possible. The layout and question level are similar to the actual exam you will sit. This means that you will be familiar with what the exam will look like, so there should be no surprises for you!

Each practice paper has a detailed marking scheme that will guide you on how the questions should/could be answered in a way that will maximise the number of marks you can achieve. Each marking scheme also includes hints and tips on how certain questions should be tackled, details of how marks are awarded and advice on what the examiners will be looking for.

How to use this book

This book can be used in two ways:

1. You can complete an entire practice paper as preparation for the final exam. If you want to use the book in this way, you can either complete a practice paper under exam conditions by setting yourself a time limit for each paper and answering it as well as possible without looking at your notes or textbooks. Or, on the other hand, you can answer questions as a revision exercise by using your notes to ensure you produce a model answer. Your teacher/lecturer may mark these for you.

2. You can use the topic index to find all the questions in the book that deal with a specific topic or unit, so that you can revise for end of topic tests and/or unit assessments. Doing it this way will allow you to focus on areas that you feel you need to work on. If you are part-way through the course, it lets you revise topics that you have previously studied and may help you identify areas you need to work on more.

The Higher course

The Higher course builds on the knowledge from the National 5 Business Management course. The main focus of the Higher course is large business – those employing more than 250 employees. The course has the following structure:

Unit 1	Understanding Business	In this Unit, you will extend your understanding of the ways in which large organisations in the private, public and third sectors operate. You will carry out activities that highlight the opportunities and constraints on these organisations in the pursuit of their strategic goals. This Unit also allows you to analyse the impact that the internal and the external environment has on an organisation's activity, and to consider the implications of these factors.

Unit 2	Management of People and Finance	In this Unit, you will develop skills and knowledge that will deepen your understanding and awareness of the issues facing large organisations in the management of people and finance. This Unit will allow you to carry out activities that will extend your grasp of relevant theories, concepts and procedures used in planning for an organisation's success, including leadership, motivation and finance. It also allows you to explain and analyse relevant business information, in each of these contexts.
Unit 3	Management of Marketing and Operations	In this Unit, you will extend the knowledge that will deepen your understanding of the importance to large organisations of having effective marketing and operations systems. The Unit will allow you to carry out activities that will extend your knowledge of relevant theories, concepts and procedures used by organisations, in order to improve and/or maintain quality and competitiveness. It will provide you with a firm understanding of the importance of satisfying both internal and external customers' needs.

(Adapted from SQA Course Specification)

Higher assessment

The Higher course is made up of two different types of assessment: Unit assessments and the Course assessment. You have to pass both types of assessment to pass the course.

Unit assessment

Each Unit will have an assessment that you have to do. The format of the Unit assessments can vary but your teacher/lecturer will advise you on what you need to do.

Unit assessments are assessed using assessment standards and ALL assessment standards need to be passed! Each assessment standard is assessed as a pass or fail only, and so you will not be given marks for these.

Course assessment

The course assessment is split into two parts:

Assignment 30% of your overall mark	This will be done in class time and is worth 30 marks. It will be sent to the SQA to be marked.
	You will be asked to research a business of your choice and will have to prepare a business report based on your findings.

Question paper 70% of your overall mark	This is done under exam conditions at the end of the course during the SQA exams and is worth 70 marks. It is set and marked by the SQA.
	The exam lasts for 2 hours and 15 minutes and has the following layout:
	Section 1 will consist of a set of short answer questions worth 30 marks. The questions will be based on a case study and other information. Most of your answers will be based on the information given.
	Section 2 will consist of FOUR extended response questions worth 10 marks EACH, so worth 40 marks overall. Each question will be based on a topic from the course – Understanding Business, People, Finance, Marketing, Operations.

Command words

In these practice papers and in the exam itself, a number of command words will be used in the questions. These command words are used to show you how you should answer a question. Some words require a longer, more detailed answer than others so it is a good idea to familiarise yourself with the command words as these will help you to answer the actual question that is being asked and will also help you structure your answer more effectively.

Command word	Meaning
Compare	Demonstrate knowledge and understanding of the SIMILARITIES and/or DIFFERENCES between things, methods, ideas or items.
Describe	Provide a statement or structure of characteristics and/or features. More than an outline or list. May refer to a concept, process, situation or facts.
Discuss	Communicate ideas and information on a subject. It may be possible to give both sides of an argument, i.e. give reasons for/against an argument.
Explain	Relate cause and effect and/or make relationships between things clear.
	Explain answers should have TWO parts – a description of something then the reason behind it.
	The IMPACT of what you are talking about must be given to fully answer an explain question.
	In the exam, EXPLAIN answers are often the ones that let learners down. The most common error is that descriptions are given instead of explanations. If you are being asked to explain something, you should be giving reasons for what you are saying. Check your answers to explain questions and make sure that you have used linking words and phrases such as 'because', 'this means that', 'therefore', 'so', 'so that', 'due to', 'since', and 'the reason is'.
Justify	Give reasons for your answer. You should be making an argument FOR the suggestions being made.

Writing in the exam

Before you start writing an answer to a question, assume that the person reading your answer knows nothing. You should explain each answer clearly and in enough detail, but without making it too wordy. Keep to the point and within the scope of the question.

In the exam you should be writing in full sentences (do not give one-word answers) and use proper written English. On the whole, bullet points should be avoided.

Knowing and using the correct business terms and words is crucial to your exam success. It may be a good idea to compile a dictionary of key business terminology in your learning journal as you go through the course. This will be a useful revision tool and will also help you when you sit the exam.

In the exam

Watch your time and pace yourself carefully. Work out roughly how much time you can spend on each answer and try to stick to this. You will have 135 minutes (2 hours 15 minutes) to answer 70 marks. This means you have approximately 1.9 minutes for every 1 mark. (Remember this includes time taken to read the case study and the questions.)

You must answer ALL the questions in Section 1 AND ALL the questions in Section 2.

Section 1, Case study, is worth 30 marks and will consist of a set of mandatory short-answer questions based on the case study. The questions will be drawn from any aspect of the Course and will require you to demonstrate the application of skills, knowledge and understanding within the context of the case study.

Section 2 is worth 40 marks and will consist of FOUR topic based MANDATORY questions.

Questions from each section will be sampled from the Course coverage, ensuring there is no duplication of topics and that there is a balanced coverage across the Course.

These practice papers will help you become familiar with the exam's instructions. It is VERY important that you follow the instructions given on the front of the examination paper, so make sure you read them carefully. When you begin the actual SQA exam, read the instructions carefully in case some things have changed.

Read each question thoroughly before you begin to answer it and make sure you know exactly what the question is asking you to do. (Remember the command words!)

Do not repeat yourself in each answer, as you will not get any more marks for saying the same thing twice. This also applies to diagrams, which will not gain you any more marks if the information is repeated within the written part of your answer. Remember to label any diagrams (e.g. product life cycle) carefully and correctly.

Exam practice and revision is the key to exam success. Everyone revises differently so find a way that works for you.

Topic Index

Exam A

Total Marks: 70

Unit	Topic	1a	1b	1c	1d	1e	1f	1g	1a	1b	1c	2a	2b	2c	3a	3b	3c	4a	4b	Marks
Unit 3 — Management of Marketing & Operations	Technology																			**22**
	Ethical & environmental										3									
	Quality	4																		
	Methods of production									3										
	Stock management								4											
	Physical evidence																			
	Process																			
	People																			
	Promotion																			
	Place																			
	Price			3																
	Product					5														
	Marketing mix																			
	Market research																			
	Customers																			
Unit 2 — Management of People & Finance	Technology															5				**23**
	Ratios							3												
	Financial statements																			
	Cash budgeting																		5	
	Sources of finance																			
	Legislation													4						
	Employee relations											2								
	Motivation & leadership																			
	Training & development																			
	Recruitment & selection												4							
Unit 1 — Understanding Business	Decision making																			**25**
	Structures				3												3			
	Stakeholders																			
	Internal factors		6																	
	External factors						6													
	Objectives																			
	Types of organisation														3					
	Role of business																	4		

Question: 1 (a, b, c, d, e, f, g) — 1 (a, b, c) — 2 (a, b, c) — 3 (a, b, c) — 4 (a, b)

Exam B — Marks grid

In the columns below, the first question number **1** covers parts a–g; the following question numbers **1, 2, 3, 4** each cover their own parts.

Unit	Subject	Topic	1a	1b	1c	1d	1e	1f	1g	1a	1b	1c	2a	2b	2c	3a	3b	3c	4a	4b	Marks
Unit 3	Management of Marketing & Operations	Technology																	5		70
		Ethical & environmental							6												
		Quality																			
		Methods of production	3																		
		Stock management																		5	
		Physical evidence																			
		Process																			
		People																			29
		Promotion											3								
		Place												4							
		Price																			
		Product																			
		Marketing mix																			
		Market research													3						
		Customers																			
Unit 2	Management of People & Finance	Technology																			
		Ratios														4					
		Financial statements		4																	
		Cash budgeting																2			
		Sources of finance															4				24
		Legislation																			
		Employee relations										2									
		Motivation & leadership								4											
		Training & development																			
		Recruitment & selection									4										
Unit 1	Understanding Business	Decision making																			
		Structures				4															
		Stakeholders																			
		Internal factors																			
		External factors																			17
		Objectives			5		3														
		Types of organisation				5															
		Role of business																			

Exam C

			Q1a	Q1b	Q1c	Q1d	Q1e	Q1f	Q1g	Q1a	Q1b	Q1c	Q2a	Q2b	Q3a	Q3b	Q3c	Q4a	Q4b	Q4c	Marks
Unit 3	**Management of Marketing & Operations**	Technology																			
		Ethical & environmental																			
		Quality				5															
		Methods of production							3												
		Stock management																			
		Physical evidence																			
		Process																			
		People																			
		Promotion																		3	
		Place																			
		Price																			
		Product																	4		
		Marketing mix																3			18
		Market research																			
		Customers																			
Unit 2	**Management of People & Finance**	Technology														4					
		Ratios					6														
		Financial statements															2				
		Cash budgeting													4						
		Sources of finance																			
		Legislation						4													34
		Employee relations																			
		Motivation & leadership			4																
		Training & development											5								
		Recruitment & selection												5							
Unit 1	**Understanding Business**	Decision making																			
		Structures								3											
		Stakeholders										2									
		Internal factors																			
		External factors									5										18
		Objectives	3	5																	
		Types of organisation																			
		Role of business																			
		Question	1							1			2		3			4			**70**

Exam D

Unit	Topic	a	b	c	d	e	f	g	h	a	b	c	a	b	c	a	b	c	a	b	Marks
Unit 3 — Management of Marketing & Operations	Technology																				
	Ethical & environmental		4																		
	Quality																			5	
	Methods of production																				
	Stock management																		5		
	Physical evidence																				
	Process																				
	People																				
	Promotion	2																			
	Place																4				
	Price																	2			
	Product															4					
	Marketing mix							4													
	Market research				4																
	Customers																				34
Unit 2 — Management of People & Finance	Technology																				
	Ratios			5																	
	Financial statements																				
	Cash budgeting																				
	Sources of finance																				
	Legislation											4									
	Employee relations									3											
	Motivation & leadership																				
	Training & development																				
	Recruitment & selection										3										15
Unit 1 — Understanding Business	Decision making													3	3						
	Structures					4															
	Stakeholders								4												
	Internal factors												4								
	External factors																				
	Objectives																				
	Types of organisation						3														
	Role of business																				21
	Question	1								1			2			3			4		**70**

Practice Papers for SQA Exams

HIGHER
BUSINESS MANAGEMENT
Exam A

Duration – 2 hours and 15 minutes

Total marks – 70

SECTION 1 — 30 marks

Attempt ALL questions.

SECTION 2 — 40 marks

Attempt ALL questions.

In your answer booklet, you must clearly identify the question number you are attempting.

Use **blue** or **black** ink.

It is recommended that you spend 15 minutes reading over the information provided in **SECTION 1** before responding to the questions.

Scotland's leading educational publishers

SECTION 1 — 30 marks

Read ALL the following information and attempt ALL the questions that follow.

The following information has been taken from the Merlin Entertainment website.

Merlin Entertainments PLC

Our Business

Merlin Entertainments plc is the largest European visitor attraction company operating in Europe, and second largest in the world to Disney. Merlin runs 106 attractions, 11 hotels and 3 holiday villages in 22 countries across four continents. Our aim is to deliver unique, memorable and rewarding experiences to millions of visitors across our growing estate. We believe that we achieve this objective largely thanks to the commitment and passion of our team and the strength of our brands, which will never fail to be distinctive, challenging and innovative.

Our Passion

We are first and foremost an entertainment company. Our passion is putting smiles (or screams) on people's faces and giving our customers memorable experiences. Through creativity and a relentless drive for excellence, we aim to immerse our visitors in our brands, constantly delighting them and enriching their understanding through fun learning. In simple terms, we love what we do!

Our Vision

Our vision is to become the worldwide leader in branded, location-based, family entertainment.

Our Company Culture – The Merlin Way

Our culture is simply 'The Merlin Way' which encapsulates our vision, values and competencies. It is at the heart of what we do. It captures what a Merlin person is about and helps shape how we will continue to achieve business growth and our objectives for the future.

The Merlin Way represents what our company is made of:

- we love what we do

- we care

- we are innovative and fast moving

- we do what we say

- we make every £, $, € ... count

- we take ownership

- …and we make it fun!

By applying The Merlin Way to all that we do, we achieve our overall aim – to deliver high quality memorable experiences to customers around the globe.

Our People – Why would you want to work for Merlin?

Our People Strategy is aligned to the business goals and defined by three key areas:

1. Employee Engagement – being the best company to work for in our industry

2. Talent & Development – nurturing our global leaders

3. Compensation and Benefits – rewarding for performance.

To ensure we focus on the areas that will add value to our employees, we conduct an annual survey, The Wizard Wants to Know, which enables us to gain honest feedback from all employees. These results are acted upon and become a key driver of continuous improvements through the engagement of our teams. Engaging with our teams and demonstrating improvement is critical to us.

Product Excellence

Our number one priority is to provide memorable experiences for every guest, from booking to departure, and all delivered within a clean and safe environment.

Product Excellence is our unique function that monitors, measures and analyses the experience of all our guests with the purpose of delivering improvement and creating competitive advantage.

We continually measure our performance via the use of on-site, real-time electronic survey kiosks and we also operate an extensive externally operated Mystery Visit programme.

We are highly competitive across our attractions which, combined with the regular use of league tables, delivers continual improvement. As a result of this focus (and a robust cultural commitment to excellence), we will continue to strive to deliver year on year improvements in customer satisfaction. In terms of monitoring feedback, we continue to take complaints very seriously – with our aim being to turn every disappointed guest into a Merlin Attractions' ambassador.

(Source: Adapted from Merlin Entertainments Website (http://www.merlinentertainments.biz/)

Further Information

Exhibit 1 — UK Brands

(Source: Adapted from Merlin Entertainments PLC Annual Report 2013)

Exhibit 2 — Extract from Merlin Entertainment's Financial Performance

	2012/2013	2011/2012	Change
	£ millions	£ millions	%
Sales	1,192	1,074	+10.9
Gross Profit	290	258	+12.3
Net Profit	186	140	+33.0

(Source: Adapted from Merlin Entertainments PLC Annual Report 2013)

Exhibit 3 — Ticket Prices for Alton Towers

Ticket	Price on the day or day before	Price when booked 2–6 days in advance	Price when booked 7 days in advance
Adult	£49.20	£44.28	£36.90
Child	£43.20	£38.88	£32.40
Family	£42.60	£38.34	£31.95
Children under 4	£0.00	£0.00	£0.00
Senior	£24.60	£22.14	£18.45

(Source: Adapted from http://www.altontowers.com/tickets)

MARKS

The following questions are based on ALL the information provided and on knowledge and understanding you have gained whilst studying the Course.

1. (a) Describe the methods of ensuring quality used by Merlin Entertainments. **4**

(b) Using examples from the case study, discuss the benefits of having a strong corporate culture. **6**

(c) Compare the pricing strategy used by Merlin Entertainments at Alton Towers with penetration pricing. **3**

(d) Merlin Entertainments have a varied product portfolio. Describe the costs and benefits of having a varied product portfolio. **5**

(e) Describe the method of grouping used by Merlin Entertainments. **3**

(f) Explain how external factors could affect Merlin Entertainments. **6**

(g) Describe suitable ratios that could be used to analyse the financial data in Exhibit 2. **3**

MARKS

SECTION 2 — 40 marks

Attempt ALL questions

1. (a) Discuss the use of Just in Time stock control. **4**

    (b) Explain the benefits of capital intensive production. **3**

    (c) Describe methods an organisation could use to be more environmentally friendly. **3**

2. (a) Describe the purpose of an appraisal. **2**

    (b) Justify the use of testing as a method of selection. **4**

    (c) Explain the impact of employment legislation on an organisation. **4**

3. (a) Compare the features of a plc with that of an organisation in the public sector. **3**

    (b) Describe sectors of industry. **4**

    (c) Define the following terms:
       • chain of command
       • delegation
       • wide span of control. **3**

4. (a) Explain the use of technology by the finance department. **5**

    (b) Describe methods of solving cash flow problems. **5**

[END OF PRACTICE QUESTION PAPER]

Practice Exam B

Practice Papers for SQA Exams

HIGHER
BUSINESS MANAGEMENT
Exam B

Duration – 2 hours and 15 minutes

Total marks – 70

SECTION 1 — 30 marks

Attempt ALL questions.

SECTION 2 — 40 marks

Attempt ALL questions.

In your answer booklet, you must clearly identify the question number you are attempting.

Use **blue** or **black** ink.

It is recommended that you spend 15 minutes reading over the information provided in **SECTION 1** before responding to the questions.

Scotland's leading educational publishers

SECTION 1 — 30 marks

Read ALL the following information and attempt ALL the questions that follow.

The following information has been taken from the website of H&M.

About Us

Our design team creates sustainable fashion for all, always at the best price. The collections include everything from dazzling party collections to the basics and functional sportswear – for women, men, teenagers and children, and for every season or occasion. In addition to clothes, shoes, bags, jewellery, make up and underwear there is also H&M Home – fashionable interiors for children and adults.

The width and variety of the H&M collections mean customers can always find something to suit their style and their wardrobe. There are H&M stores in 54 markets worldwide, and online shopping in 12 countries.

H&M designs its own products, has no middlemen, buys the right product from the right market in large volumes, has efficient logistics and is cost conscious in every part of the business. H&M's designers, pattern makers and buyers work in teams to create the collections. Flexible planning of the product range and quick decision-making ensure that the collections are continually adapted to what customers want.

Corporate Social Responsibility

Climate change is one of the major challenges of our time. Like many others, we have a keen interest in taking action to tackle this – and also a responsibility to do so. Being 'climate smart' is about making an ongoing series of choices, big and small. For us, that can mean anything from choosing more efficient lighting for our stores, to working with our suppliers to help them reduce their CO_2 emissions.

- We've increased our in-store electricity efficiency by 14% since 2007.

- 18% of our electricity comes from renewable sources, like wind power. Our goal is 100%.

- We also have our own solar panels. Last year, these generated enough energy to supply 145 European households for an entire year.

Transport, packaging, hangers and shopping bags are all part of the retail business. That said, efficient material use and the application of smart methods to reuse and recycle means we can reduce waste and – one day – get rid of it altogether.

We're committed to reducing, reusing and recycling wherever we can. In our vision of a better fashion future, nothing gets wasted. To achieve this vision, we'll need to inspire everyone who's connected to our business – from our suppliers to our customers – to be a part of the journey.

It breaks our heart to see fashion end up in landfill. So, as the first fashion company in the world, we've launched a global initiative that means customers can hand in unwanted garments – from any brand and in any condition – to H&M stores.

Ethical Behaviour

Fair play, respect and integrity are fundamental to our business. Being ethical also means protecting human rights and providing an inclusive business environment. And not only to take responsibility for our colleagues, but also to serve as a good example wherever we operate.

Our business touches the lives of millions of people around the world. We believe every single one of those interactions should be guided by mutual respect, integrity, transparency and honesty.

When it comes to making ethical business decisions, we are committed to respecting human rights, taking a clear stand against any form of corruption and embracing diversity and inclusion.

- 50% of our board members are women.

- We've adopted the UN Guiding Principles on Business and Human rights.

- We teamed up with Civil Rights Defenders to support human rights and equality.

- We've started with mandatory training on Code of Ethics for all concerned employees, at the end of 2013, 60% had attended the training.

(Source: Adapted from H&M's Website (http://about.hm.com))

Further Information

Exhibit 1 — Extract from H&M's Financial Performance

	2013	**2012**
	£ (000)	**£ (000)**
Fixed Assets	26,488	22,941
Current Assets	39,188	37,232
TOTAL ASSETS	**65,676**	**60,173**
Current Liabilities	17,397	14,010
Long Term Liabilities	3,031	2,328
TOTAL LIABILITIES	**20,428**	**16,338**
NET WORTH	**45,248**	**43,835**

(Source: Adapted from H&M Annual Results 2013)

Exhibit 2 — H&M Grouping Information

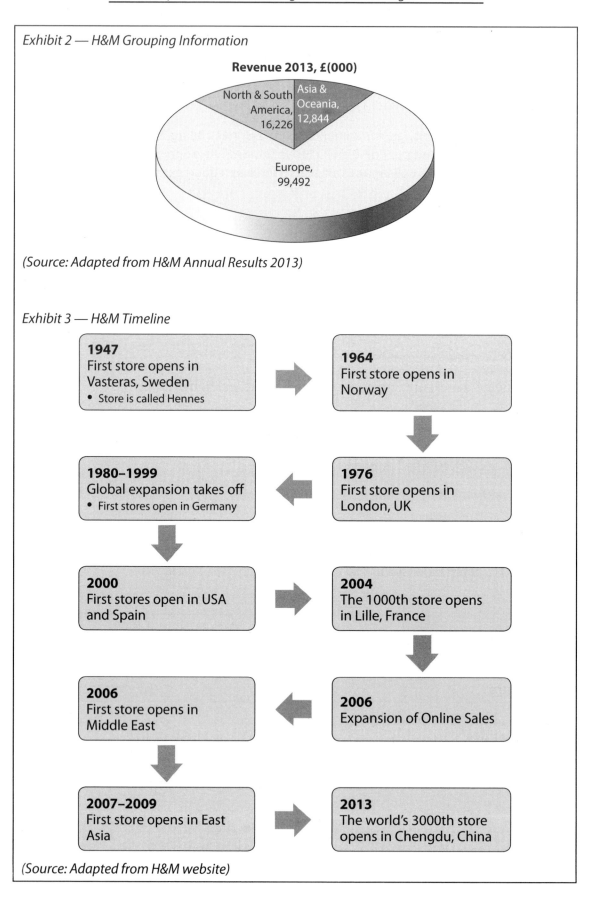

Revenue 2013, £(000)

North & South America, 16,226

Asia & Oceania, 12,844

Europe, 99,492

(Source: Adapted from H&M Annual Results 2013)

Exhibit 3 — H&M Timeline

1947
First store opens in Vasteras, Sweden
- Store is called Hennes

1964
First store opens in Norway

1980–1999
Global expansion takes off
- First stores open in Germany

1976
First store opens in London, UK

2000
First stores open in USA and Spain

2004
The 1000th store opens in Lille, France

2006
First store opens in Middle East

2006
Expansion of Online Sales

2007–2009
First store opens in East Asia

2013
The world's 3000th store opens in Chengdu, China

(Source: Adapted from H&M website)

MARKS

The following questions are based on ALL the information provided and on knowledge and understanding you have gained whilst studying the Course.

1. (a) Justify the method of production that H&M would use.   3

   (b) Discuss the use of the financial statement shown in Exhibit 1.   4

   (c) Describe ways H&M have shown they have good Corporate Social Responsibility.   5

   (d) Compare the method of grouping used in Exhibit 2 with product grouping.   4

   (e) Discuss the advantages and disadvantages of H&M being a multinational.   5

   (f) Describe the method of growth used by H&M.   3

   (g) Using examples from the case study, explain the benefits to H&M of operating ethically.   6

MARKS

SECTION 2 — 40 marks

Attempt ALL questions

1. (a) Compare two theories of motivation. **4**

(b) Discuss internal and external recruitment. **4**

(c) Describe ways of ensuring good employee relations. **2**

2. (a) Discuss methods of promotion an organisation could use. **3**

(b) Explain why an organisation may choose to sell its products using a wholesaler. **4**

(c) Compare two methods of market research. **3**

3. (a) Describe how an organisation could improve their liquidity. **4**

(b) Justify sources of finance suitable for a large organisation. **4**

(c) Explain the benefits of using a cash budget. **2**

4. (a) Discuss the role of technology in the operations department. **5**

(b) Describe factors that would need to be considered when choosing a channel of distribution. **5**

[END OF PRACTICE QUESTION PAPER]

Practice Exam C

Practice Papers for SQA Exams

HIGHER
BUSINESS MANAGEMENT
Exam C

Duration – 2 hours and 15 minutes

Total marks – 70

SECTION 1 — 30 marks

Attempt ALL questions.

SECTION 2 — 40 marks

Attempt ALL questions.

In your answer booklet, you must clearly identify the question number you are attempting.

Use **blue** or **black** ink.

It is recommended that you spend 15 minutes reading over the information provided in **SECTION 1** before responding to the questions.

Scotland's leading educational publishers

SECTION 1 — 30 marks

Read ALL the following information and attempt ALL the questions that follow.

The following information has been taken from the Volkswagen Group website.

About Us

The Volkswagen Group with its headquarters in Wolfsburg, Germany, is one of the world's leading automobile manufacturers and the largest carmaker in Europe. In 2013, the Group increased the number of vehicles delivered to customers to 9.731 million (2012: 9.276 million).

In Western Europe, almost one in four new cars (24.8 percent) is made by the Volkswagen Group. Group sales revenue in 2013 totalled €197 billion (2012: €193 billion), while profit after tax amounted to €9.3 billion (2012: €21.9 billion).

Brands & Products

The Group comprises twelve brands from seven European countries: Volkswagen Passenger Cars, Audi, SEAT, ŠKODA, Bentley, Bugatti, Lamborghini, Porsche, Ducati, Volkswagen Commercial Vehicles, Scania and MAN.

Each brand has its own character and operates as an independent entity on the market. The product spectrum ranges from motorcycles to low-consumption small cars and luxury vehicles. In the commercial vehicle sector, the products include ranges from pick-ups, buses and heavy trucks.

The Volkswagen Group is also active in other fields of business, manufacturing large-bore diesel engines for marine and stationary applications (turnkey power plants), turbochargers, turbomachinery (steam and gas turbines), compressors and chemical reactors. It also produces vehicle transmissions, special gear units for wind turbines, slide bearings and couplings as well as testing systems for the mobility sector.

In addition, the Volkswagen Group offers a wide range of financial services, including dealer and customer financing, leasing, banking and insurance activities, and fleet management.

Global Situation

The Group operates 106 production plants in 19 European countries and a further eight countries in the Americas, Asia and Africa. Every weekday, 572,800 employees worldwide produce some 39,350 vehicles, and work in vehicle-related services or other fields of business. The Volkswagen Group sells its vehicles in 153 countries.

The Group's goal is to offer attractive, safe and environmentally sound vehicles which can compete in an increasingly tough market and set world standards in their respective class.

Equal Opportunities

Different cultural traditions in the global markets and increasing economic dynamism demand great flexibility from a modern company. To achieve this, it is necessary to make maximum use of the opportunities and innovative potential that stem from the employees' different backgrounds. Staff appreciation has long been a tradition in the Volkswagen Group. The same thing applies to the specific promotion of socially disadvantaged groups. We attach great value to the diversity of the different people we employ. Mutual respect is a principle that has been written into our Group values. It forms the basis for a productive corporate climate in which all employees enjoy the same opportunities.

Valued Diversity

Not all members of staff are equal. There are outward and subjective differences, different lifestyles and different ideas about the future. Productively exploiting this diversity within the workforce is one of the goals of our management.

Career Women

Ever since the 1980s, the Volkswagen Group has been encouraging and promoting equality between men and women. Targeted measures are employed to boost the proportion of women even further and to make us even more attractive on our way to being the top employer.

(Source: Adapted from Volkswagen Group Website (http://www.volkswagenag.com/content/ vwcorp/content/en/homepage.html))

Further Information

Exhibit 1 — Extract from Volkswagen Group's Financial Performance

	2013	2012
	%	%
Net Profit %	6.3	13.2
Return on Capital (Automotive)	14.5	16.6

(Source: Adapted from Volkswagen Group Annual Report 2013)

Exhibit 2 — *Volkswagen Group, Number of Employees*

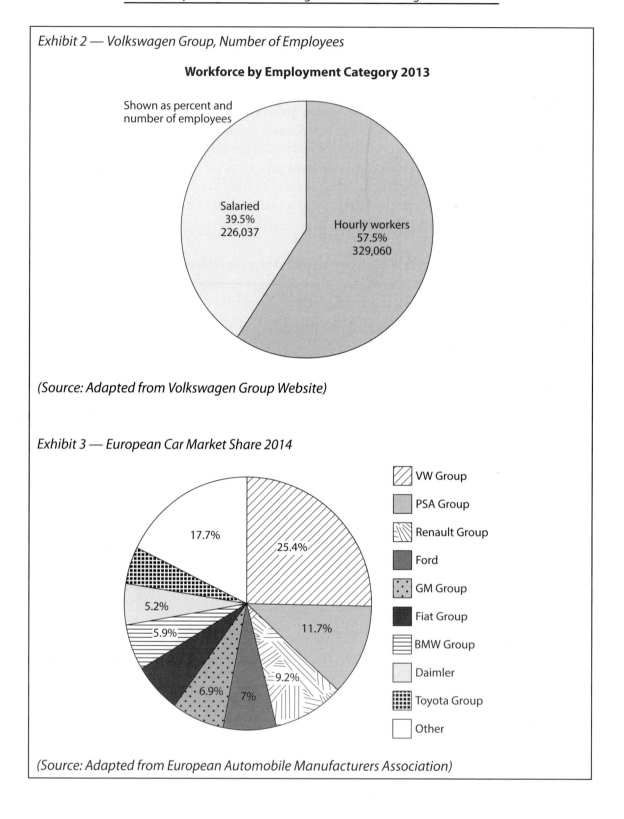

Workforce by Employment Category 2013

Shown as percent and number of employees

Salaried
39.5%
226,037

Hourly workers
57.5%
329,060

(Source: Adapted from Volkswagen Group Website)

Exhibit 3 — *European Car Market Share 2014*

- VW Group
- PSA Group
- Renault Group
- Ford
- GM Group
- Fiat Group
- BMW Group
- Daimler
- Toyota Group
- Other

17.7%

25.4%

5.2%

5.9%

11.7%

6.9%

7%

9.2%

(Source: Adapted from European Automobile Manufacturers Association)

MARKS

The following questions are based on ALL the information provided and on knowledge and understanding you have gained whilst studying the Course.

1. (a) Describe possible objectives for VW Group. **3**

(b) Discuss the method of growth used by VW Group. **5**

(c) Compare the methods of motivating staff used in Exhibit 2. **4**

(d) Describe methods VW Group could use to ensure quality. **5**

(e) Explain why the ratios shown in Exhibit 1 have changed. **6**

(f) Using examples from the case study, describe how VW Group are complying with workplace legislation. **4**

(g) Justify the production method used by VW Group. **3**

MARKS

SECTION 2 — 40 marks

Attempt ALL questions

1. (a) Compare tall and flat organisation structures.   **3**

   (b) Explain the impact of Government Economic Policy on an organisation.   **5**

   (c) Describe the interdependence between the owners and employees of an organisation.   **2**

2. (a) Discuss the use of work-based qualifications.   **5**

   (b) Justify the use of workforce planning.   **5**

3. (a) Describe the limitations of financial information.   **4**

   (b) Explain the use of technology by the finance department.   **4**

   (c) Compare two final accounts prepared by the finance department.   **2**

4. (a) Describe the elements of the extended marketing mix.   **3**

   (b) Explain what happens to profitability at stages in the product life cycle.   **4**

   (c) Describe out of the pipeline promotions that an organisation could use.   **3**

[END OF PRACTICE QUESTION PAPER]

Practice Exam D

Practice
Papers for
SQA Exams

HIGHER
BUSINESS MANAGEMENT
Exam D

Duration – 2 hours and 15 minutes

Total marks – 70

SECTION 1 — 30 marks

Attempt ALL questions.

SECTION 2 — 40 marks

Attempt ALL questions.

In your answer booklet, you must clearly identify the question number you are attempting.

Use **blue** or **black** ink.

It is recommended that you spend 15 minutes reading over the information provided in **SECTION 1** before responding to the questions.

Scotland's leading educational publishers

SECTION 1 — 30 marks

Read ALL the following information and attempt
ALL the questions that follow.

The following information has been taken from the 2013 Annual Report of British Airways plc.

British Airways Profile

British Airways is the UK's largest international airline and one of the world's leading global premium carriers. Its principal place of business is London, the world's largest premium travel market. BA's main home at Heathrow is Terminal 5, which has been voted the world's Best Airport Terminal by airline travellers across the globe in the latest SkyTrax survey.

Operating one of the most extensive international scheduled airline route networks, together with its joint business agreement, codeshare and franchise partners, BA flies to more than 70 different countries. BA carries almost 40 million customers a year and has a fleet of more than 280 aircraft.

BA is a founding member of **one**world, the alliance of airlines around the globe, which together serves some 800 destinations in 150 countries

BA's vision is to be the most admired airline. They will do this by delivering outstanding service to engaged customers which, together with strong cost control, will make them financially fit and enable continued investment in great people, great products and the best network.

Growth in the UK

The BA brand had a successful year in 2013 maintaining the high level brand scores achieved in 2012 when the airline played a significant role in the London 2012 Olympic and Paralympic Games.

In the well-respected Superbrands survey of 2013, BA was the second ranked business brand behind Apple. For consumer superbrands, BA was ranked number one in 2014 and came fourth in 2013, behind Rolex, Microsoft and Apple. We were also named the top airline brand of the year.

BA overtook Virgin Atlantic to become Britain's favourite carrier, according to a YouGov survey. The market research company uses surveys to measure the public perception of hundreds of brands every day, drawing its data from seven different measurement systems. Furthermore, figures from BrandIndex, which independently measures the perception of thousands of brands, show that BA led the way among airlines when it came to customer consideration.

The airline has also received numerous awards throughout the year, including: best short-haul airline in the Telegraph Travel Awards, and best airline for customer service in the British Travel Awards.

Setting the Standard for Responsible Aviation

BA continues to lead the industry in adopting a responsible approach to the environmental impact of aviation. This is not only imperative for the environment, but is the right financial approach when faced with high fuel costs, and it is an increasingly important consideration for customers.

The airline is working to establish Europe's first sustainable bio-jet plant with US energy company Solena Fuels Corporation, which is expected to power some of BA's planes from around 2017. The airline has committed to purchasing sustainable fuel from the plant.

Community Investment

In 2010, BA launched Flying Start, a charity partnership with Comic Relief. The aim was ambitious — to raise £6 million and change the lives of children worldwide.

(Source: Adapted from British Airways Annual Report 2013)

Further Information

Exhibit 1 — Promotions

(Source: Adapted from www.dontpayful.com)

BA Loyalty Scheme

(Source: Adapted from www.tmgcorporate.com)

Exhibit 2 — Corporate Structure

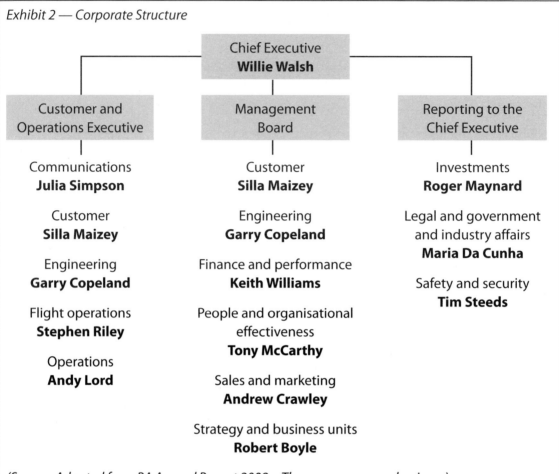

(*Source: Adapted from BA Annual Report 2009 – The way we run our business*)

Exhibit 3 — Extract from British Airway's Financial Performance

	2012/2013	2011/2012	Change
	£ millions	£ millions	%
Sales	11,421	10,827	+5.5
Gross Profit	708	233	+203.9
Net Profit (after tax)	284	114	+149.1

(*Source: Adapted from British Airways PLC Annual Report 2013*)

MARKS

The following questions are based on ALL the information provided and on knowledge and understanding you have gained whilst studying the Course.

1. (a) Describe the methods of promotion used in Exhibit 1.   **2**

   (b) Discuss, using examples from the case study, the benefits of BA being environmentally friendly.   **4**

   (c) Explain the change in the Net Profit and Gross Profit for 2013.   **5**

   (d) Justify the method of market research used in the case study.   **4**

   (e) Discuss the features of the organisation structure shown in Exhibit 2.   **4**

   (f) Explain the benefits of BA being a plc.   **3**

   (g) Describe how the extended marketing mix is used by BA.   **4**

   (h) Discuss the interdependence and conflict of stakeholders from the information provided.   **4**

MARKS

SECTION 2 — 40 marks

Attempt ALL questions

1. (a) Discuss the institutions involved in employee relations.   **3**

   (b) Describe the costs and benefits of advertising a job vacancy online.   **3**

   (c) Explain the impact of the Equality Act on an organisation.   **4**

2. (a) Describe the internal factors that can impact an organisation.   **4**

   (b) Compare the types of decisions a manager could make.   **3**

   (c) Discuss the use of SWOT analysis as a tool to aid decision making.   **3**

3. (a) Describe ways of extending the life cycle of a product.   **4**

   (b) Explain the benefits of using e-commerce.   **4**

   (c) Justify the use of loss-leaders.   **2**

4. (a) Discuss factors that need to be considered to ensure effective stock management.   **5**

   (b) Describe methods of ensuring quality.   **5**

[END OF PRACTICE QUESTION PAPER]

Answers

General Marking Principles for Higher Business Management

This information is provided to help you understand the general principles that must be applied when the SQA mark responses to questions in the exam paper. These principles must be read in conjunction with the detailed marking instructions for each paper, which identify the key features required in the responses.

a) Marks for each response must **always** be assigned in line with these general marking principles and the mark schemes for each assessment.

b) Marking should always be positive. This means that, for each response, marks are accumulated for the demonstration of relevant skills, knowledge and understanding: they are not deducted from a maximum on the basis of errors or omissions.

c) For each response, the following provides an overview of the marking principles. Refer to the specific mark scheme for further guidance on how these principles should be applied.

Marks will be awarded as follows for:

(i) Questions that ask you to **Describe** …

You must make a number of relevant factual points, which may be characteristics and/or features, as appropriate to the question asked. These points may relate to a concept, process or situation.

You may provide a number of straightforward points or a smaller number of developed points, or a combination of these.

Up to the total mark allocation for this question:

- **1 mark** should be given for each relevant factual point.

- **1 mark** should be given for any further development of a relevant point, including exemplification when appropriate.

(ii) Questions that ask you to **Explain** …

You must make a number of accurate relevant points that relate cause and effect and/or make the relationships clear. These points may relate to a concept, process or situation.

You may provide a number of straightforward points of explanation or a smaller number of developed points, or a combination of these.

Up to the total mark allocation for this question:

- **1 mark** should be given for each relevant point of explanation.

- **1 mark** should be given for a further development of a relevant point, including exemplification when appropriate.

(iii) Questions that ask you to **Compare** …

You must demonstrate knowledge and understanding of the similarities and/or differences between things, methods or choices, for example. The relevant comparison points could include theoretical concepts.

Up to the total mark allocation for this question:

- 1 mark should be given for each accurate point of comparison.

(iv) Questions that ask you to **Discuss** …

You must make a number of points that communicate issues, ideas, or information about a given topic or context that will make a case for and/or against. It is not always necessary to give both sides of the debate in responses.

Up to the total mark allocation for this question:

- **1 mark** should be given for each accurate point of knowledge that is clearly relevant.

- **1 mark** should be given for any further development of a relevant point, including exemplification or a conclusion when appropriate.

(Adapted from the SQA Higher Business Management Specimen Question Paper)

Marking Scheme for Exam A

Section 1

Question		Expected Answer(s)	Max Mark	Additional Guidance
1	(a)	Responses could include the following: Quality Management (QM) • Every employee in Merlin is involved in ensuring every guest has a memorable experience from booking to departure. • QM should result in higher level of customer satisfaction. Mystery Shoppers • Merlin uses mystery visitors — a member of the public is trained to act as a normal guest when they are actually evaluating their experience. • Feedback is then given to Merlin about how the 'guest' found the experience and the service. Benchmarking • Merlin use league tables across their attractions. • Applies a set of benchmarks that each attraction must strive to achieve.	4	Candidates' responses must relate directly to quality methods from the case study. Award **1 mark** for each valid description. Award **1 mark** for each development point up to a maximum of **2**.

Question		Max Mark	Additional Guidance
1	**(b)** Responses could include the following:	**6**	Award **1 mark** for each valid discussion point.
	• Employees feel they are part of the organisation and belong to it; this can provide them with a sense of security and can improve motivation.		Award **1 mark** for each valid development point.
	• It can motivate staff, which in turn will lead to improved efficiency and higher productivity.		Accept any other suitable response.
	• It can create positive relationships within the organisation that will enable better communication and decision-making.		*TOP TIP*
	• Employee loyalty can be increased, which will decrease staff turnover and staff absence rates.		A description of corporate culture is not asked for here, so no marks will be awarded for writing a description.
	• The image and identity of the organisation can be improved, which will be visible to all stakeholders.		
	• Customer loyalty might be higher because they associate themselves with the identity (e.g. logos, uniform and attraction design) of the organisation. It may also be recognisable across the globe if it is a multinational organisation.		
	• There will be consistency across the organisation, which will allow employees to work in different locations or branches if necessary.		

Question		Expected Answer(s)	Max Mark	Additional Guidance
1	(c)	Responses could include the following: • Promotional pricing is when prices are lowered for a short period of time before raising to their normal price again, whereas penetration pricing is used until a product becomes more well known. • Promotional pricing is used for already established products whereas penetration pricing is used when a new product is launched on to the market. • Discrimination pricing charges different prices for the same product depending on when it is bought, whereas penetration pricing charges the same price until the product becomes well known. • Both discrimination/promotional and penetration encourage customers to buy the product when the prices are low.	3	Award **1 mark** for each direct comparison. Accept any other suitable response. *HINT* A direct comparison must be made to achieve a mark.
1	(d)	Responses could include the following: Costs • Advertising costs can be high, as the business has to make sure that all their products are advertised. • It can be expensive to continually research and develop new products to keep a large portfolio. • One product may cause a problem that can affect the whole portfolio. Benefits • Increased profits from selling a variety of products. • It is easier to increase brand awareness. • New products can be launched easily as they will be recognised.	5	Award **1 mark** for each valid description. Award **1 mark** for each valid development point. Accept any other suitable response.

Question		Expected Answer(s)	Max Mark	Additional Guidance
		• A range of products spreads the risk of failure.		
		• It is easy to cope with changes in demand or seasonal demand.		
		• A wider market can be targeted with different products.		
1	(e)	Responses could include the following:	3	Award **1 mark** for each valid description.
		Product Grouping		Award **1 mark** for each valid development point.
		• The organisation is structured around the products it sells/service it provides.		Accept any other suitable response.
		• Each department concentrates on a specific product/service. For example: The Dungeons, Alton Towers, Sealife and Madame Tussauds.		
		• Each department is able to respond quickly to changes in the market.		
		• If a product isn't performing well this is easily identified to managers.		
1	(f)	Responses could include the following:	6	Award **1 mark** for each valid explanation point.
		• Changes to the law could mean that Merlin have to change their policies and procedures to comply with the new laws.		Award **1 mark** for each valid development point.
		• A tax increase would mean that guests would have less disposable income to spend at Merlin attractions.		Accept any other suitable response.
		• If government environmental targets were introduced, steps would need to be taken by Merlin to comply with the new targets or they could be fined.		*HINT* The IMPACT of each point must be stated for a mark to be awarded.
		• If unemployment is high, people will be cautious about spending money on days out, so may not go to any of the Merlin attractions.		
		• If interest rates increase and Merlin is relying on loans, it could mean that they experience cash flow problems.		

(continued)

Question		Expected Answer(s)	Max Mark	Additional Guidance
		Changes could occur in trends and fashion, so Merlin will need to carry out market research to ensure it keeps up to date with what people want.		
		Merlin will need to have family-friendly policies in place to deal with people who want to work on a flexible basis.		
		Merlin needs to keep up to date with weather forecasts, as good/bad weather will increase/decrease the number of visitors to their attractions. Staffing levels would need to be adjusted accordingly.		
		If a competitor opens a new attraction, Merlin will have to try and stay ahead of the competition by offering lower prices and a better customer experience, or they could lose customers to the competition.		
1	(g)	Responses could include the following:	3	Award **1 mark** for each valid description.
		Gross Profit		Award **1 mark** for each valid development point.
		The Gross Profit % (GP%) shows the amount of profit a business has made from buying and selling stock.		Accept any other suitable response.
		The higher the GP% the better.		
		The GP% shows the amount of gross profit made from each £ of sales.		
		Net Profit		
		Net Profit % (NP%) shows the amount of profit the business has made after paying all the expenses.		
		The higher the % the more profit is being made.		
		The NP% shows the amount of net profit that is being made from each £ of sales.		
		If the NP% is very low in comparison to the GP%, it could indicate that expenses are too high.		

Section 2

Question		Expected Answer(s)	Max Mark	Additional Guidance

1	(a)	Responses could include the following:
		
		Advantages
		
		• less warehouse space is needed
		  – reduced rent costs
		• capital is not tied up in stock so can be used elsewhere
		• order must be placed before production starts
		  – reduced waste as less stock is stored
		  – reduced risk from changes in fashion/trends
		• reduced theft as stock is easier to monitor.
		
		Disadvantages
		
		• dependent on reliable suppliers
		  – if stock does not arrive then production will stop
		  – may not have time to check the quality of stock before production starts
		• increased number of delivery charges
		  – increased administration costs
		• may lose out on economies of scale/bulk buying discounts.
			4	Award **1 mark** for each valid discussion point.
				
				Award **1 mark** for each valid development point.
				
				Candidates do not need both advantages and disadvantages to attract full marks.
				
				Accept any other suitable response.

Question		Expected Answer(s)	Max Mark	Additional Guidance
1	(b)	Responses could include the following: • Machines can work 24/7. This means more products can be made. • Machines produce a better quality of product as they don't make mistakes. This means that there will be less customer complaints. • Machines can work faster than humans. This leads to increased efficiency and productivity. • Machines don't get bored of repetitive tasks. This means there will be a consistent standard across all products.	3	Award **1 mark** for each valid explanation point. Award **1 mark** for each valid development point. Accept any other suitable response. *HINT* The IMPACT of each point must be stated for a mark to be awarded.
1	(c)	Responses could include the following: Recycling • Encourage employees to use recycling bins. • Reuse materials in the production process. Reducing Packaging • Use only the amount of packaging needed. • Cuts down on costs. • Use environmentally friendly packaging. Operate a Fair Trade Policy • Use suppliers that have produced or obtained raw materials in an ethical manner.	3	Award **1 mark** for each valid description. Award **1 mark** for each valid development point. Accept any other suitable response.

Question		Expected Answer(s)	Max Mark	Additional Guidance
		<u>Minimise Waste</u> • Ensure employees are trained well so no human error occurs. • Ensure machinery is kept in good condition to avoid errors. • Do not 'dump' waste in landfill if it can be recycled. • Dispose of waste in an environmentally-friendly manner.		
2	(a)	Responses could include the following: Appraisals are used to • assess employees' performance in their post • identify employees' strengths and highlight any areas of concern so that effective training or other support can be given • improve employee motivation and performance • identify any promotional possibilities.	2	Award **1 mark** for each valid description. Award **1 mark** for each valid development point. Accept any other suitable response.
2	(b)	Responses could include the following: • Psychometric tests can be used to establish if someone would fit in to a particular culture. • Used to confirm what an applicant has stated on their application form/CV. • Test results of each candidate can be compared. • Skills and abilities can be confirmed. • Competencies can be compared against the essential and desirable criteria for the job.	4	Award **1 mark** for each valid point. Award **1 mark** for each valid development point. Accept any other suitable response. *TOP TIP* A description of testing methods is not asked for here, so no marks will be awarded for writing a description.

Question		Expected Answer(s)	Max Mark	Additional Guidance
2	(c)	Responses could include the following:	4	Award **1 mark** for each valid explanation point.
		Equality Act 2010		Award **1 mark** for each valid development point.
		• When job adverts are created, managers need to ensure they have not been discriminatory in the wording of the advert or this could lead to prosecution.		Accept any other suitable response.
		• Any physical barriers that would stop someone from accessing the building need to be considered and dealt with; ramps, lifts, etc installed, or this could lead to the business being taken to court.		*HINT* The IMPACT of each point must be stated for a mark to be awarded.
		• All employees of a business need to be aware of legislation and what they need to do to comply with it so they don't break the law.		
		Employment Rights Act 1996		*TOP TIP* A description of the legislation is not asked for here, so no marks will be awarded for writing a description.
		• Employers must provide a written statement of employment or they risk being taken to court by the employee.		
		• Employees have the right to a pay slip, so employers will need to keep a record of pay or they could be fined.		
		• Employees have a right not to be unfairly dismissed. So employers will need to have policies in place covering dismissal, to ensure that they don't unfairly dismiss an employee and end up in court.		
		National Minimal Wage Act 1998		
		• Employers must pay the legal minimum wage depending on the age of the employee. Failure to do so would result in the organisation being fined.		
		• This may mean an organisation has to budget carefully to ensure it can afford the wage costs or the organisation may not be able to pay the wages.		

Question		Expected Answer(s)	Max Mark	Additional Guidance
3	(a)	Responses could include the following: • A plc is owned by shareholders, WHEREAS an organisation in the public sector is owned by the government. • A plc is financed through the selling of shares, WHEREAS an organisation in the public sector is financed through taxes. • A plc is controlled by a board of directors, BUT a public sector organisation is controlled by the government. • A plc aims to maximise profits, HOWEVER a public sector organisation aims to use taxes efficiently.	3	Award **1 mark** for each direct comparison. Accept any other suitable response. *HINT* A direct comparison must be made to achieve a mark.
3	(b)	Responses could include the following: • Primary sector — extract material from the ground. Includes agriculture, fishing, oil, gas and mining. • Secondary sector — manufacturing goods. Takes raw materials and transforms them into finished products. Includes builders, bakers and car manufacturers. • Tertiary sector — provide a service. Provided by people who have been trained. Includes personal trainers, hotels and supermarkets. • Quaternary sector — provide knowledge-based and information services. Includes consultants, ICT and computing and education.	4	Award **1 mark** for each description. Award **1 mark** for each valid development point. Minimum of TWO sectors must be described to achieve full marks. Accept any other suitable response.

Question		Expected Answer(s)	Max Mark	Additional Guidance
3	(c)	Responses could include the following:	3	Award **1 mark** for each correct description given.
		• Chain of command is the order in which instructions are passed down in an organisation from one level of management to another. A long chain of command may mean communication and decision making takes longer, compared to a short chain of command.		No marks should be awarded for development points.
		• Delegation is one of the functions of management and takes place when someone requests a task to be completed by a subordinate. This could be because the senior staff member doesn't have the time or because the subordinate is more skilled in the task.		Accept any other suitable response.
		• Wide span of control relates to the number of subordinates who report to a manager. It can be difficult to manage as the manager has a lot of staff to oversee.		
4	(a)	Responses could include the following:	5	Answers MUST relate to the FINANCE department. Do not accept answers about any other department.
		Spreadsheets		
		• Perform 'what if' scenarios — by changing projected sales figures, the finance department can see the effect on profits.		Award **1 mark** for each valid explanation point.
		• Produce graphs and charts — easy to identify any changes in profits over a period of time.		Award **1 mark** for each valid development point.
		• Formulae calculations are carried out instantly and accurately — beneficial when preparing financial statements.		TWO different types of software must be explained to achieve full marks.
		• Formulae are amended automatically when the spreadsheet is amended.		
		• Formulae can be replicated — saves time.		

Question	Expected Answer(s)	Max Mark	Additional Guidance
	Word		Accept any other suitable response.
	• Can be used to produce financial reports for shareholders — graphs and charts can be inserted in to word processed documents. THIS MEANS THAT the shareholder can get all the information they need in an easy to read and professional format.		**HINT**
	Accounting Packages		The IMPACT of each point must be stated for a mark to be awarded.
	• Used to calculate payroll, track credit transactions and produce Cash Budgets, Financial Statements and Ratio Analysis.		**TOP TIP**
	• One of the benefits of dedicated software is that a suite of specialised reports can be embedded within the system. THIS MEANS THAT reports that are relevant to the business can be produced quickly and accurately.		A description of technology is not asked for here, so no marks will be awarded for writing a description.
	• Increase the speed of decision making.		
	• These systems can also link into external bodies, such as HM Revenue and Customs. This allows the electronic submission of forms, such as VAT returns. This process will remove human error from the submission process, as it is an automatic submission from the system.		
	Cloud Accounting/Computing		
	• Organisations do not physically possess the software in their premises but simply access it on a rental basis from a remote site. This reduces short-term costs with no need for a dedicated server and will ensure that accounting data is backed up.		
	• Organisations can store their data in 'the cloud'. This means that the data can be accessed from anywhere and is usually backed up so there is less chance of it becoming lost or corrupt.		

Question		Max Mark	Expected Answer(s)	Additional Guidance
4	(b)	**5**	Responses could include the following:	Award **1 mark** for each correct description given.
			• Reduce purchases (*raw materials*) to reflect falling sales.	Award **1 mark** for each development point.
			• Find a cheaper supplier of raw materials.	At least THREE methods must be described to achieve full marks.
			• Encourage debtors, those who have bought sales on credit, to pay quicker by offering cash discounts.	Accept any other suitable response.
			• Take advantage of the full credit period to delay paying for purchases.	
			• Encourage sales by advertising.	
			• Arrange loans just before they are needed.	
			• Rent or lease new machinery rather than buy it.	
			• Reduce wage costs by	
			— reducing working hours	
			— banning overtime payments	
			— changing payment system to be based on sales	
			— terminating employment contracts, e.g. temporary staff	
			— moving production to another country with cheaper costs.	

Marking Scheme for Exam B

Section 1

Question		Expected Answer(s)	Max Mark	Additional Guidance
1	(a)	Responses could include the following: • Batches can be changed to suit the requirements of the customer, which results in higher customer satisfaction. • Raw materials can be bought in bulk therefore saving money. • Cost savings can be made, as standardised machinery is used. • The need for highly skilled workers is reduced.	3	Award **1 mark** for each valid justification. No marks for development points. Accept any other suitable response.
1	(b)	Responses could include the following: • it shows the value of an organisation at a particular point in time • how much the organisation owns • how much the organisation owes • how much net profit was made by the organisation • the value of dividends paid to shareholders.	4	Award **1 mark** for each valid discussion point. Award **1 mark** for each valid development point. Accept any other suitable response.

Question		Expected Answer(s)	Max Mark	Additional Guidance
1	(c)	Responses could include the following: • employees have equal opportunities • suppliers are treated fairly • increasing electricity efficiency • have their own solar panels • local communities are respected and supported • take environmental responsibilities seriously • take ethical responsibilities seriously • reduction in carbon footprint by using waste management strategies — reduce, reuse, recycle.	5	Award **1 mark** for each valid description. Award **1 mark** for each valid development point. Accept any other suitable response.
1	(d)	Responses could include the following: • Product grouping structures an organisation's activities around products, WHEREAS geographical grouping structures activities around specific locations. • Geographical grouping ensures the needs of local customers can be met, HOWEVER product grouping does not take the needs of locals into account. • BOTH product and geographical grouping allow an organisation to respond quickly to changes in the market. • BOTH can have duplication of resources.	4	Award **1 mark** for each direct comparison. Accept any other suitable response. *HINT* A direct comparison must be made to achieve a mark.

Question		Expected Answer(s)	Max Mark	Additional Guidance
1	(e)	Responses could include the following:	5	Award **1 mark** for each valid discussion point.
		Advantages		At least one advantage and one disadvantage must be discussed to achieve full marks.
		• Economies of scale can be taken advantage of, thereby reducing costs.		
		• Legal restrictions can be avoided in other countries compared to the home country.		Award **1 mark** for each valid development point.
		• They may be able to take advantage of different tax regulations in other countries, thereby increasing profitability.		Accept any other suitable response.
		• Expanding abroad will mean the organisation becomes bigger, increasing sales, and also safer from takeovers by other organisations.		
		• Government grants that do not require to be paid back might be given in some countries for locating there.		
		• Resources, e.g. labour, might be cheaper in some countries, reducing the overall expenses.		
		Disadvantages		
		• Each country's laws need to be complied with, which might mean changes need to be made to the goods or service, and these might be expensive.		
		• The culture might vary from one country to another and the organisation will need to consider this.		
		• Language barriers may make trading more difficult and expensive if language interpreters need to be employed.		
		• Language barriers may also mean that communication is misinterpreted and incorrect decisions made.		

SQA Exams: Higher Business Management Marking Scheme for Exam B

Question		Expected Answer(s)	Max Mark	Additional Guidance
1	(f)	Responses could include the following: • Organic growth happens when an organisation increases the number of goods and services it offers. • It also happens when the organisation increases the number of outlets and employees that it has. • This will help to increase sales. • It increases profit.	3	Award **1 mark** for each valid description. Award **1 mark** for each valid development point. Accept any other suitable response.
1	(g)	Responses could include the following: • Supports local charities THEREFORE shows empathy towards needy causes. • Supports community projects. This could lead to increased trust from customers. • Employees treated fairly so this will mean they are more loyal and more motivated. • Adhering to ethical practices could increase sales. • Being honest could lead to increased customer loyalty and therefore could increase sales/profits. • Suppliers are treated fairly.	6	Award **1 mark** for each valid explanation point. Accept any other suitable response. *HINT* The IMPACT of each point must be stated for a mark to be awarded.

Section 2

Question	Expected Answer(s)	Max Mark	Additional Guidance
1 (a)	Responses could include the following: • Taylor states that employees are only interested in money, WHEREAS Mayo claims they need social interaction. • Taylor states that employees are only interested in money, WHEREAS Maslow states that employees have five needs that need to be met at work. • Herzberg believed that a job should be enhanced by empowering employees, WHEREAS Taylor claimed that employees needed larger tasks broken down into smaller, repetitive tasks. • BOTH Mayo and Maslow believed that employees needed more than just money to motivate them at work.	4	Award **1 mark** for each direct comparison. Accept any other suitable response. *HINT* A direct comparison must be made to achieve a mark.
1 (b)	Responses could include the following: Internal Recruitment • involves appointing existing employees to new positions within the business • includes promotion • no external advertising fees • staff members are already known to the organisation • less training is required • no fresh blood is brought in to the organisation.	4	Award **1 mark** for each valid discussion point. Both internal and external recruitment need to be discussed to achieve full marks. Award **1 mark** for each valid development point. Accept any other suitable response.

(continued)

Question		Expected Answer(s)	Max Mark	Additional Guidance
		External Recruitment		
		• involves appointing a new employee from outwith the organisation		
		• jobs are advertised externally		
		• anyone can apply for the job		
		• wider range of applicants		
		• new ideas are brought in to the organisation		
		• high costs of advertising externally		
		• existing staff may feel aggrieved if an external candidate gets the job		
		• more training needed for new employees.		
1	(c)	Responses could include the following:	2	Award **1 mark** for each valid description.
		• Works council — Enables the employees to be consulted and involved in the decision-making process of the business.		Award **1 mark** for each valid development point.
		• Team working — Employees are given the opportunity to work with others in teams or on specific projects. They share decision making, successes and failures. They learn from each other and build trust and respect.		Accept any other suitable response.
		• Staff training — Leads to increased efficiency and a higher rate of staff retention.		
		• Communication — Employees value their opinions being listened to but equally they do not usually have difficulty following instructions, provided they are kept informed of decisions and the reasons why they have been made.		

Question		Expected Answer(s)	Max Mark	Additional Guidance
		• Support systems — Many businesses and organisations have a separate Human Resources department or section that is able to give a range of support to employees, e.g. this can take the form of counselling for stress or bereavement. They may have in place absent management procedures where employees are encouraged to take part in 'return to work' interviews or 'phased' return to work after a long absence. They may offer a range of 'family friendly' policies such as flexible working or working from home.		
		• Quality circles — Groups of volunteer employees who meet to discuss issues of improvements in the business.		
		• Employee of the month and achievement awards — Many businesses operate schemes whereby employees can receive awards, bonuses or recognition for their role in the business. It can be a competition type event or based on feedback from customers and colleagues.		
2	(a)	Responses could include the following: Into the Pipeline Promotions These are aimed at retailers who agree to sell the finished products from the manufacturer. There are a number of different promotions, as follows:	3	Award **1 mark** for each valid discussion point. To achieve full marks, both methods have to be discussed. Accept any other suitable response.
		• Dealer promotions and loaders, such as prizes given to the retailer that sells the most of the product or extra products given for volume, e.g. one free box of sweets for every five boxes stocked.		
		• Point of sale displays including posters, stands, free samples.		
		• Staff training on the product features and advantages, so that they can deal confidently with consumers who are purchasing.		
		• Extended credit given to enable retailers to purchase stock.		

(continued)

Question	Expected Answer(s)	Max Mark	Additional Guidance
	Out of the Pipeline Promotions		
	These are aimed at consumers in order to persuade them to buy products. There are a number of different promotions, as follows:		
	• discounts		
	• special offers — such as buy one get one free		
	• free samples or tasting		
	• price reductions, e.g. 65p off for a limited period only		
	• loyalty cards		
	• celebrity endorsement		
	• vouchers or coupons		
	• free entry into competitions		
	• these promotions are effective in the short term as they attract the consumer's attention.		
2	(b) Responses could include the following:	**4**	Award **1 mark** for each valid explanation point.
	• Distribution and storage costs are reduced because products might be bought in bulk.		Award **1 mark** for each valid development point.
	• The wholesaler may promote the manufactured product, resulting in less cost for the manufacturer.		Accept any other suitable response.
	• The risk of not selling the product to a retailer or to the customer is taken on by the wholesaler, and therefore risk for the manufacturer is reduced.		

Question	Expected Answer(s)	Max Mark	Additional Guidance
	• Packaging, labelling and marketing might be carried out by the wholesaler.		*HINT* The IMPACT of each point must be stated for a mark to be awarded.
	• The manufacturer does not have to worry about having to sell excess stock if there are changes in the business environment (e.g. fashion).		
	• The wholesaler may provide information on the product for the retailer.		*TOP TIP* A description of a wholesaler is not asked for here, so no marks will be awarded for writing a description.
	• Retailers do not have to pay for expensive storage facilities to hold stock, as they can buy smaller quantities, compared to sourcing directly from the manufacturer.		
2 (c)	Responses could include the following:	3	Award **1 mark** for each direct comparison.
	• Field research is carried out by an organisation for their own purpose, WHEREAS desk research is information that already exists.		Accept any other suitable response.
	• Field research is expensive to carry out, BUT desk research is fairly cheap in comparison.		
	• Desk research can be carried out quickly, BUT this is not so for field research.		*HINT* A direct comparison must be made to achieve a mark.
	• Field research ensures the information gathered is relevant and accurate, WHEREAS desk research could contain lots of unnecessary information.		
	• BOTH desk and field research allow an organisation to find out what the customer thinks about their products.		
	• BOTH desk and field research will allow an organisation to tailor adverts to different market segments.		

Question		Expected Answer(s)	Max Mark	Additional Guidance
3	(a)	Responses could include the following: • reduce theft or breakages of stock • increase current assets • decrease current liabilities • use JIT stock management.	4	Award **1 mark** for each valid description. Award **1 mark** for each valid development point. Accept any other suitable response.
3	(b)	Responses could include the following: Selling Shares • only available to limited companies on the stock market • large sum of money is raised • have limited liability. Venture Capitalists • available when other lenders consider the organisation too risky • sometimes come with expertise and advice. Leasing • no initial large investment • any faults, breakdowns or maintenance are usually covered by the lease agreement • organisation given most up-to-date models when they are released.	4	Award **1 mark** for each valid justification. No marks for development points. Accept any other suitable response. *TOP TIP* A description of sources of finance is not asked for here, so no marks will be awarded for writing a description.

Question		Expected Answer(s)	Max Mark	Additional Guidance
		Mortgage		
		• can secure a large amount of money		
		• long period for repayment.		
		Retained Profits		
		• no interest charged		
		• no increase/change in ownership.		
3	(c)	Responses could include the following:	2	Award **1 mark** for each valid explanation point.
		• It shows whether the business will have a surplus (more cash expected to come in than will go out) or deficit (more cash expected to go out than will come in). THIS MEANS THAT the business can take corrective action.		Award **1 mark** for each valid development point.
		• It shows whether additional finance is required to ensure the business continues to operate effectively SO the business can arrange a loan.		Accept any other suitable response.
		• It helps control expenses by highlighting periods when expenses could be high. This lets the business ensure they have the funds available.		*HINT* The IMPACT of each point must be stated for a mark to be awarded.
		• It helps to make decisions, e.g. whether to launch into a new product area.		*TOP TIP* A description of a cash budget is not asked for here, so no marks will be awarded for writing a description.
		• It measures performance of departments. Could be used as a target for the organisation and different departments within the organisation to work towards.		

Question		Expected Answer(s)	Max Mark	Additional Guidance
4	(a)	Responses could include the following:	5	Award **1 mark** for each valid discussion point.
		Technology can be used in a number of different ways in the operations function.		Award **1 mark** for each valid development point.
		• Computer facilities (e.g. computer and internet) can be used for purchasing materials online.		Accept any other suitable response.
		• E-mail can be used to confirm an order has been received and to let the customer know about the progress and status of the order (e.g. when it has been dispatched).		
		• Websites can be used to compare the prices of different suppliers before deciding which one to purchase.		
		• Deliveries can be tracked and traced via the websites of logistical companies.		
		• Computer programs (e.g. a database or spreadsheet) can be used to store stock levels.		
		• EPOS can provide automatic updates on stock and sales levels.		
		• Computer-aided design (CAD) can be used in the research and design stage of a new product before it is manufactured.		
		• Computer-aided manufacture (CAM) involves using computer-controlled equipment and robots.		
4	(b)	Responses could include the following:	5	Award **1 mark** for each valid description.
		• reliability of other organisations		Award **1 mark** for each valid development point.
		• legal restrictions		Accept any other suitable response.
		• availability of finance		
		• the product being distributed		
		• the image associated with the product		
		• the stock management system being used		
		• the distribution capability of the manufacturer.		

Marking Scheme for Exam C

Section 1

Question		Expected Answer(s)	Max Mark	Additional Guidance
1	(a)	Responses could include the following: • survival — to continue trading • profit — to have more income than costs • customer satisfaction — to make customers happy so they return • market leader — to become the biggest business in the market.	3	Award **1 mark** for each valid description. Award **1 mark** for each valid development point. Accept any other suitable response.
1	(b)	Responses could include the following: • Organic growth — this happens within a single organisation where growth comes from opening more branches, taking on more workers or increasing the number of products it sells, etc. • Diversification — when a business operates in a new/different market. This reduces risk and can allow for increased profits.	5	Award **1 mark** for each valid discussion point. Award **1 mark** for each valid development point. Accept any other suitable response.
1	(c)	Responses could include the following: • A salary is a set yearly rate whereas with an hourly rate, the more hours you work, the more you get paid. • Salaried staff members don't usually get paid for overtime, so a salary does not encourage staff to work longer hours. • Staff paid an hourly rate usually earn time and a half or double time for overtime, so this gives them the incentive to work extra hours. • Staff paid a salary sometimes get extra fringe benefits that would help increase their motivation — mobile, laptop, car, house, etc.	4	Award **1 mark** for each direct comparison. Accept any other suitable response. *HINT* A direct comparison must be made to achieve a mark.

Question		Expected Answer(s)	Max Mark	Additional Guidance
1	(d)	Responses could include the following:	5	Award **1 mark** for each valid description.
		Quality Management		Award **1 mark** for each valid development point.
		• This involves every employee in the organisation ensuring that quality is built in at each and every stage of the production process.		Accept any other suitable response.
		• It is an overall business philosophy designed to ensure customer satisfaction.		
		• It ensures that quality raw materials are purchased from reliable suppliers.		
		• Any errors or problems in the production process are eliminated and the failure rate of finished products is very low indeed.		
		Mystery Shoppers		
		• This can be used to gauge the quality of a product or a service.		
		• Typically a member of the public is trained to act as a 'normal' shopper, when in fact they are analysing and evaluating their shopping experience or the quality of the product.		
		• The employees of the business are unaware that this is taking place, so very important and accurate feedback can be received about the customer experience.		
		Benchmarking		
		• Benchmarking is an approach to quality that involves the business applying a set of standards, or benchmarks.		
		• The business has to make sure that it achieves these benchmarks in order to stay competitive.		

Question	Expected Answer(s)	Max Mark	Additional Guidance
	Quality Circles		
	• This involves bringing groups of employees together with the management in order to discuss issues of quality.		
	• Employees are usually trained to identify, analyse and solve some of the problems in their work. They would then present solutions to management, and where possible, implement solutions themselves.		
	• One of the aims is to give employees more responsibility and increased motivation.		
	Quality Control		
	• This involves checking products after they have been produced to make sure they meet the standards expected.		
	• If a product fails the quality check it is discarded or recycled back into the production process.		
	• Quality control can be wasteful if it is only carried out at the end of the production process.		
	Quality Assurance		
	• This involves a planned and systematic approach to checking products at more regular intervals during the production process and trying to avoid problems happening in the first place.		
	• Quality assurance involves the whole production process, i.e. starting with good quality raw materials.		
	• If quality assurance checks are carried out, employees are more confident that the completed product will be acceptable to customers.		

Question		Expected Answer(s)	Max Mark	Additional Guidance
1	(e)	Responses could include the following: The net profit (NP) ratio has decreased — • The gross profit (GP) has gone down so the net profit will go down. • Sales have gone down. This will decrease the GP and therefore decrease the NP. • Purchases have increased. This will decrease the NP. • Stock has been lost due to theft. More purchases would have to be made, therefore decreasing NP. • Expenses have increased, therefore decreasing NP. The return on capital has decreased — • Sales have decreased due to less advertising, or customers moving to a competitor. This will decrease the return on capital employed (RCE). • Expenses are higher. This will decrease the NP and therefore the RCE.	6	Award **1 mark** for each valid explanation point. Accept any other suitable response. *HINT* The IMPACT of each point must be stated for a mark to be awarded. *TOP TIP* A description of the ratios is not asked for here, so no marks will be awarded for writing a description.
1	(f)	Responses could include the following: • employing staff from different cultural backgrounds so as not to be discriminatory on grounds of ethnicity • employing women • valuing diversity • paying the minimum wage to hourly rate employees • exploiting diversity.	4	Award **1 mark** for each valid description. Award **1 mark** for each valid development point. Accept any other suitable response.

Question		Expected Answer(s)	Max Mark	Additional Guidance
1	(g)	Responses could include the following: Flow Production • Large amounts of identical products can be made. • Machines can work 24 hours a day, 365 days a year. • Economies of scale can be achieved as raw materials can be bought in bulk. • Quality can be checked at various points in the production process.	3	Award **1 mark** for each valid justification. No marks for development points. Accept any other suitable response. *TOP TIP* A description of the production methods isn't asked for here, so no marks will be awarded for writing a description.

Section 2

Question		Expected Answer(s)	Max Mark	Additional Guidance
1	(a)	Responses could include the following: • Tall structures have many layers of management, WHEREAS flat structures only have a few layers of management. • Tall structures have a long chain of command, WHEREAS flat structures have a short chain of command. • Tall structures are often found in the public sector, BUT flat structures are often found in small organisations. • Flat structures have a wide span of control, BUT a tall structure has a narrow span of control.	3	Award **1 mark** for each direct comparison. Accept any other suitable response. *HINT* A direct comparison must be made to achieve a mark.
1	(b)	Responses could include the following: • Banks across the world have restricted lending. THIS MEANS THAT an organisation could find it difficult to get a loan to enable them to grow or buy a new asset. • Government spending has been cut. This means organisations are less likely to sell goods to public sector organisations, so could result in a fall in sales. • Inflation being kept low COULD MEAN THAT there is a fall in demand for goods and services. • Interest rates being kept low MEANS THAT customers are not encouraged to save money so this could increase sales and therefore profits. • Government provided state aid given to some organisations results in them surviving. • Quantitative easing provides new money to the economy, which stimulates spending.	5	Award **1 mark** for each valid explanation point. Accept any other suitable response. *HINT* The IMPACT of each point must be stated for a mark to be awarded.

Question		Expected Answer(s)	Max Mark	Additional Guidance
1	(c)	Responses could include the following: • Owners need employees to carry out different tasks and employees need owners to pay their wages. • Owners need employees to be as productive as they can and employees need owners to provide the necessary job training.	2	Award **1 mark** for each valid description. Award **1 mark** for each valid development point. Accept any other suitable response.
2	(a)	Responses could include the following: Advantages • a recognised qualification can be gained • training often takes place on the job • assessment is carried out by a qualified assessor • the organisation benefits from having skilled staff. Disadvantages • time-consuming to complete • some people might not want to complete a qualification • costs money to enter someone for a qualification.	5	Award **1 mark** for each valid discussion point. Award **1 mark** for each valid development point. Accept any other suitable response.
2	(b)	Responses could include the following: • From the strategic aims of the organisation, plans can be made for when new staff will be required. • Analysis of the labour market allows an organisation to foresee any shortages in the specially qualified staff.	5	Award **1 mark** for each valid justification. No marks for development points. Accept any other suitable response.

(continued)

Question		Expected Answer(s)	Max Mark	Additional Guidance
		• Analysing the demand for the business lets an organisation determine how many employees they are likely to need in the future. • Analysis of the existing workforce allows training needs to be identified. • Analysis of the existing workforce allows an organisation to plan for people retiring and how their experience should be replaced.		*TOP TIP* A description of workforce planning isn't asked for here, so no marks will be awarded for writing a description.
3	(a)	Responses could include the following: • The figures are based on historic data and while past performance is a good indicator of future performance, it is only a guide. • Making comparisons between different organisations can be difficult because there are often many differences, e.g. size. • External factors (PESTEC) are not taken into account. • No consideration is taken of what stage the product being sold is at in the Product Life Cycle. • Only financial information is considered and so human resources are not factored in. For example, the recent retirement of an effective Chief Executive Officer (CEO) would be ignored. Staff motivation and morale are also ignored. • New product developments are ignored.	4	Award **1 mark** for each valid description. Award **1 mark** for each valid development point. Accept any other suitable response.

Question		Expected Answer(s)	Max Mark	Additional Guidance
3	(b)	Responses could include the following: Spreadsheets • Perform 'what if' scenarios — by changing projected sales figures, the finance department can see the effect on profits. • Produce graphs and charts — easy to identify any changes in profits over a period of time. • Formulae calculations are carried out instantly and accurately — beneficial when preparing financial statements. • Formulae are amended automatically when the spreadsheet is amended. • Formulae can be replicated — saves time. Word • Can be used to produce financial reports for shareholders — graphs and charts can be inserted in to word-processed documents. THIS MEANS THAT the shareholder can get all the information they need in an easy to read and professional format. Accounting Packages • Used to calculate payroll, track credit transactions and produce Cash Budgets, Financial Statements and Ratio Analysis. • One of the benefits of dedicated software is that a suite of specialised reports can be embedded within the system. THIS MEANS THAT reports that are relevant to the business can be produced quickly and accurately.	4	Award **1 mark** for each valid explanation point. Accept any other suitable response. *HINT* The IMPACT of each point must be stated for a mark to be awarded.

(continued)

Question	Expected Answer(s)	Max Mark	Additional Guidance
	• Increases the speed of decision making. • These systems can also link into external bodies, such as HM Revenue and Customs. This allows electronic submission of forms, such as VAT returns. This process will remove human error from the submission process, as it is an automatic submission from the system. Cloud Accounting/Computing • Organisations do not physically possess the software in their premises but simply access it on a rental basis from a remote site. This reduces short-term costs with no need for a dedicated server and will ensure that accounting data is backed up. • Organisations can store their data in 'the cloud'. This means that the data can be accessed from anywhere and is usually backed up so there is less chance of it becoming lost or corrupt.		
3 (c)	Responses could include the following: • The balance sheet shows how much a business is worth, WHEREAS a profit and loss account shows how much profit an organisation has made. • The balance sheet shows how many assets the organisation has, WHEREAS the profit and loss account lists all the expenses of the organisation. • Both the balance sheet and the profit and loss account are prepared at the end of the financial year. • Both the balance sheet and profit and loss account are used in ratio analysis.	2	Award **1 mark** for each direct comparison. Accept any other suitable response. *HINT* A direct comparison must be made to achieve a mark.

Question		Expected Answer(s)	Max Mark	Additional Guidance
4	(a)	Responses could include the following: • Process — The different processes and systems used to deliver the service being provided. • People — Those involved in providing the service to customers, e.g. staff. • Physical evidence — The location of where the service is being offered and what it looks like, e.g. store layout and design.	3	Award **1 mark** for each valid description. Award **1 mark** for each valid development point. Accept any other suitable response.
4	(b)	Responses could include the following: • Development — No sales so high costs and no profits. • Introduction — Sales are low and costs are still high. This means there is very little profit if any at all. • Growth — Sales grow rapidly. This means profits begin to increase. • Maturity — Sales are stable and profits are high. • Saturation — High profits before they start to decline. • Decline — Sales fall therefore profits fall and a loss will eventually be incurred.	4	Award **1 mark** for each valid explanation point. Accept any other suitable response. **HINT** The IMPACT of each point must be stated for a mark to be awarded.
4	(c)	Responses could include the following: • discounts • special offers — buy one get one free • free samples or tasting • price reductions, e.g. 65p off for a limited period only • loyalty cards • celebrity endorsement • vouchers or coupons • free entry into competitions.	3	Award **1 mark** for each valid description. Award **1 mark** for each valid development point. Accept any other suitable response.

Marking Scheme for Exam D

Section 1

Question		Expected Answer(s)	Max Mark	Additional Guidance
1	(a)	Responses could include the following: • Special offers are usually short term and on selected products, e.g. buy one get one free, 3 for 2, etc. • Loyalty schemes — collect points for making purchases. The points can then be used to obtain vouchers or a discount on future purchases.	2	Award **1 mark** for each valid description. Award **1 mark** for each valid development point. Accept any other suitable response.
1	(b)	Responses could include the following: • Working to establish a bio-jet plant. This will reduce the carbon footprint of BA. • Working on purchasing sustainable fuel from the plant. This will help reduce the amount of waste produced by BA. • Community investment with Flying Start will help improve the image of BA. • Giving money to charities worldwide will also help improve the image of BA.	4	Award **1 mark** for each valid discussion point. Award **1 mark** for each valid development point. Accept any other suitable response.
1	(c)	Responses could include the following: • Higher sales due to increased volume or increased selling price — this results in a higher GP and NP. • Lower cost of sales — cheaper supplier means that purchases are reduced. This results in a higher GP and NP. • Increase in marketing activities — this will increase sales and therefore increase GP and NP.	5	Award **1 mark** for each valid explanation point. Award **1 mark** for each valid development point. Accept any other suitable response.

Question		Expected Answer(s)	Max Mark	Additional Guidance
		• Better quality product being sold, thereby attracting more customers — this will increase sales due to higher demand and/or higher selling price due to higher quality. The result of this is higher GP and NP. • Expenses being lower will result in a higher NP.		*HINT* The IMPACT of each point must be stated for a mark to be awarded.
1	(d)	Responses could include the following: Survey • primary research • first-hand information is gathered • fit for purpose • clarification can be gained • can be completed at a time that suits • people can be spread across a large geographical area if a postal survey is used • phone surveys can be less expensive than personal interviews.	4	Award **1 mark** for each valid justification. No marks for development points. Accept any other suitable response. *TOP TIP* A description of the methods is not asked for here, so no marks will be awarded for writing a description.
1	(e)	Responses could include the following: Flat Structure • few layers of management • short chain of command • instructions are quickly passed down • wide span of control • few opportunities for promotion.	4	Award **1 mark** for each valid discussion point. Award **1 mark** for each valid development point. Accept any other suitable response.

Question		Expected Answer(s)	Max Mark	Additional Guidance
1	(f)	Responses could include the following: • Limited liability for shareholders so they only lose what was initially invested. • More sources of finance available so they can get money easier to allow growth, etc. • Can take advantage of economies of scale so they can save money by buying supplies cheaper. • Bigger organisations can have more power in the marketplace as they control more of it.	3	Award **1 mark** for each valid explanation point. Award **1 mark** for each valid development point. Accept any other suitable response. *HINT* The IMPACT of each point must be stated for a mark to be awarded.
1	(g)	Responses could include the following: Process • Important because customers expect the service they receive to be efficient and reliable. • For example, when you place an order at a fast food 'drive thru' counter, you expect to receive the order within a very short period of time. • New ways of providing a service have to be offered to customers through, for example, smartphones and tablet computers. • Businesses have to keep monitoring their processes and updating them where necessary to make sure customers receive what they expect. People • Important because customers expect to receive a high quality service.	4	At least **TWO** elements must be discussed to achieve full marks. If only one element discussed, max of 2 marks. Award **1 mark** for each valid description. Award **1 mark** for each valid development point. Accept any other suitable response.

Question	Expected Answer(s)	Max Mark	Additional Guidance
	• Making sure the correct people are employed and then trained is important in achieving this. • Rewarding them and encouraging them to work hard is also important. Physical Evidence • Important because it helps a customer to distinguish one organisation from another. • It includes the layout, design and facilities available within a store or where the service is being provided. • Customers are unlikely to purchase from a business if physical evidence is poor.		
1 (h)	Responses could include the following: • BA shareholders are dependent on the management to make the most profitable decisions. • Poor-performing BA employees, e.g. pilots, cabin crew, will let management down. • Employees need guidance and instructions from their managers. • Customers rely on employees to provide a good quality service. • BA want to pay as low a wage as possible but employees want a high wage for their work. • BA want high profits but customers want cheap prices. • Cabin crew want customers to spend as much money as possible, but customers want as much discount as they can get.	4	Award **1 mark** for each valid discussion point. Award **1 mark** for each valid development point. Candidates do not need both advantages and disadvantages to attract full marks. Accept any other suitable response.

Section 2

Question		Expected Answer(s)	Max Mark	Additional Guidance
1	(a)	Responses could include the following: Trade Unions • A trade union is an organisation that employees can join to help them negotiate better pay and conditions. • A trade union will advise union members and help resolve disputes with employers. • The trade union may also offer additional benefits to its employees such as financial services and legal advice. ACAS (Advisory, Conciliation and Arbitration Service) • When industrial disputes cannot be resolved, businesses will often ask for direct help from an organisation called ACAS. • ACAS provides information, advice, training, conciliation and other services for employers and employees to help prevent or resolve workplace problems. • Their overall aim is to improve employee relations and to prevent disputes from arising in the first place or escalating after they have begun. • Often ACAS provides 'arbitration' whereby both sides in the dispute ask for an agreement to be reached to which they can both adhere.	3	Award **1 mark** for each valid discussion point. Award **1 mark** for each valid development point. Both Trade unions and ACAS need to be discussed to achieve full marks. Accept any other suitable response.
1	(b)	Responses could include the following: Benefits • potential candidates can apply for the job at any time of the day	3	Award **1 mark** for each valid description. Award **1 mark** for each valid development point.

Question	Expected Answer(s)	Max Mark	Additional Guidance
	• wider pool of potential candidates		Accept any other suitable response.
	• reduces advertising costs.		
	Costs		
	• a more thorough selection process may be needed, which can be expensive		
	• there is a chance the wrong person is given the job, as an external candidate is unknown to the organisation		
	• could attract a high volume of time-wasters, as applying online is often easier to do.		
1 (c)	Responses could include the following: Equality Act 2010 • When job adverts are created, managers need to ensure they have not been discriminatory in the wording of the advert. • Any physical barriers that would stop someone from accessing the building need to be considered. This means that ramps, lifts, etc may need to be installed at a high financial cost. • All employees of a business need to be aware of legislation and what they need to do to comply with it, so policy documents will need to be drawn up and issued to all staff. This costs money and time. • If an employee feels they are being discriminated against, the organisation has a duty of care. This means they will have to investigate it and take action where necessary. This takes time and costs money.	4	Award **1 mark** for each valid explanation point. Award **1 mark** for each valid development point. Accept any other suitable response. *HINT* The IMPACT of each point must be stated for a mark to be awarded. *TOP TIP* A description of the equality act is not asked for here, so no marks will be awarded for writing a description.

Question		Expected Answer(s)	Max Mark	Additional Guidance
2	(a)	Responses could include the following:	**4**	Award **1 mark** for each valid description.
		Finance		Award **1 mark** for each valid development point.
		• There may not be enough finance to make new purchases:		Accept any other suitable response.
		– this could cause production to stop		
		– this could lead to orders being delayed		
		– customers would then become unhappy.		
		• A lack of finance could also mean that objectives are not being met, e.g. growth.		
		Employees		
		• Employees may not have the correct skills to carry out a task/job, so the quality of the work may be poor.		
		• Employees may not be motivated to carry out a job.		
		• Customers would be put off by the poor quality workmanship.		
		• Low motivation could result in high absences.		
		Management		
		• Managers may not have enough experience or skill in decision making.		
		• Could result in poor decisions being made.		
		• This could impact the whole organisation, leading to lower sales/profits.		

Question	Expected Answer(s)	Max Mark	Additional Guidance
	<u>Existing Technology</u>		
	• Current technology may be out of date so the production process may not be as effective as it could be.		
	• If old machinery breaks down, production stops and this could result in orders not being met and therefore unhappy customers.		
	• An organisation may not be able to keep up with competitors if they are unable to use social media to advertise or sell their products.		
2 (b)	Responses could include the following: • Strategic decisions are long term decisions, WHEREAS tactical decisions are medium term, WHEREAS operational decisions are short term (day to day). • Strategic decisions are made by senior managers, WHEREAS tactical decisions are made by middle management, WHEREAS operational decisions are made by team leaders/supervisors. • Strategic decisions are the aims of the organisation, WHEREAS tactical decisions help to achieve the aims.	3	Award **1 mark** for each direct comparison. Accept any other suitable response. *HINT* A direct comparison must be made to achieve a mark.
2 (c)	Responses could include the following: • The process draws together Strengths, Weaknesses, Opportunities and Threats. • Strengths identify the areas that are going well and might include things such as a highly qualified management team, large financial reserves, strong market share or patents and copyrights. They are areas over which the business has some control.	3	Award **1 mark** for each valid discussion point. Award **1 mark** for each valid development point. Accept any other suitable response.

(continued)

Question	Expected Answer(s)	Max Mark	Additional Guidance
	• Strengths will be used to gain a competitive advantage for the business.		
	• Weaknesses represent the issues within an organisation that can cause the business to be vulnerable to competition. These might include out of date equipment, an unmotivated workforce or cash flow problems.		
	• Weaknesses are areas ripe for improvement.		
	• Opportunities should be exploited to give the organisation a competitive edge. Examples include deregulation of the market, developments in technology or lifestyle changes.		
	• Threats are any things that can adversely affect a business and could include potential rises in inflation, recession or potential competition.		
	• Attempts should be made to match Strengths with Opportunities and convert Weaknesses into Strengths.		
3 (a)	Responses could include the following:	4	Award **1 mark** for each valid description.
	• Changing the appearance of the packaging to give the product a new image.		Award **1 mark** for each valid development point.
	• Changing the size, variety or shape of the product, as this makes it different from the original.		Accept any other suitable response.
	• Improving the quality of the finished product by, for example, using higher quality raw materials.		
	• Changing the method of promotion used to promote the product, for example, by offering a discount.		
	• Changing the method of advertising the product to reach a larger number of people.		

Question		Expected Answer(s)	Max Mark	Additional Guidance
		• Changing the price of the product (up or down), to reach a different market segment.		
		• Changing the place the product is sold, for example, offering it online as well as in a shop.		
		• Changing the name of the product.		
		• Changing the use of the product so that it can be used for a different purpose.		
3	(b)	Responses could include the following:	4	Award **1 mark** for each valid explanation point.
		• Customers worldwide can purchase goods therefore reaching a larger number of customers.		Award **1 mark** for each valid development point.
		• Customers can buy online 24/7 from their own home so this should increase sales.		Accept any other suitable response.
		• Online discounts may be available as a shop is not required. This should attract more customers.		*HINT* The IMPACT of each point must be stated for a mark to be awarded.
		• Product information can be updated and accessed quickly. This means all product information should be accurate.		
		• Products can be compared with others allowing a customer to make a fully informed decision.		*TOP TIP* A description of e-commerce is not asked for here, so no marks will be awarded for writing a description.
		• It is convenient if access to a retailer is not available, so customers unable to get to a retailer will buy the product.		
		• Stock availability can often be checked instantly and products reserved. This will save the customer valuable time travelling to a retailer to find the product out of stock.		
		• A website can be set up fairly cheaply. This will save the organisation money.		

Question		Expected Answer(s)	Max Mark	Additional Guidance
3	(c)	Responses could include the following: • Attracts customers in to the shop. • Encourages customers to purchase other products that are priced normally. • Profit is made on the total amount of purchases the customer makes.	2	Award **1 mark** for each valid justification. No marks for development points. Accept any other suitable response. *TOP TIP* A description of loss-leaders is not asked for here, so no marks will be awarded for writing a description.
4	(a)	Responses could include the following: <u>Maximum Stock Level</u> • The highest amount of stock that can be stored at one time. • At this level stock costs will be at the minimum per unit because the organisation is at full capacity. <u>Minimum Stock Level</u> • The lowest amount of stock that should be stored at one time. • At this level there is a danger that stock levels could fall too low and production would stop. <u>Re-order Level</u> • The quantity at which more stock is ordered.	5	Award **1 mark** for each valid discussion point. Award **1 mark** for each valid development point. Three factors need to be discussed to achieve full marks. Accept any other suitable response.

Question		Expected Answer(s)	Max Mark	Additional Guidance
		Re-order Quantity		
		• The quantity of stock that has to be ordered to bring levels back to the maximum stock level.		
		Lead Time		
		• The time that passes between ordering stock and it arriving.		
4	(b)	Responses could include the following:	5	Award **1 mark** for each valid description.
		A quality product involves		Award **1 mark** for each valid development point.
		• using high quality raw materials		Accept any other suitable response.
		• training employees regularly and to a high standard		
		• using up-to-date machinery and equipment		
		• using appropriate packaging		
		• the product being delivered on time		
		• being produced to quality standards, e.g. Kitemark.		
		Quality Circles		
		• This involves groups of employees coming together with the management in order to discuss issues of quality.		
		• Employees are usually trained to identify, analyse and solve some of the problems in their work. They would then present solutions to management, and where possible, implement solutions themselves.		
		• One of the aims is to give employees more responsibility and increased motivation.		

(continued)

Question	Expected Answer(s)	Max Mark	Additional Guidance
	Quality Control		
	• This involves checking products after they have been produced to make sure they meet the standards expected.		
	• If a product fails the quality check, it is discarded or recycled back into the production process.		
	• Quality control can be wasteful if it is only carried out at the end of the production process.		
	Quality Assurance		
	• This involves a planned and systematic approach to checking products at more regular intervals during the production process and trying to avoid problems happening in the first place.		
	• Quality assurance involves the whole production process, i.e. starting with good quality raw materials.		
	• If quality assurance checks are carried out, employees are more confident that the completed product will be acceptable to customers.		
	Total Quality Management		
	• This involves every employee in the organisation ensuring that quality is built in at each and every stage of the production process.		
	• It is an overall business philosophy designed to ensure customer satisfaction.		
	• It ensures that quality raw materials are purchased from reliable suppliers.		
	• Any errors or problems in the production process are eliminated and the failure rate of finished products is very low indeed.		

Question	Expected Answer(s)	Max Mark	Additional Guidance
	• All staff, including office staff, are involved in the quality process.		
	• Often organisations have quality awards for their high standards, e.g. Investors in People, Charter Marks, Kitemarks.		
	• Customers can therefore see that the product is good quality.		
	Quality Standards and Symbols		
	• In the UK, there are recognised systems of quality standards, e.g. The British Standards Institute which places a Kitemark on products that meet the standard.		
	• British Standards cover a wide range of businesses and products.		
	• Other standards include ISO 9001, which is an international standard for Quality Management.		
	Benchmarking		
	• Benchmarking is an approach to quality that involves the business applying a set of standards or benchmarks.		
	• The business has to make sure that it achieves these benchmarks in order to stay competitive.		
	• Benchmarking can be internal or external.		
	• Internal benchmarking involves setting standards within the organisation that are then used to compare performance across different departments.		
	• External benchmarking involves setting standards within the industry against which each business can be measured.		

(continued)

Question	Expected Answer(s)	Max Mark	Additional Guidance
	Mystery Shopping • The use of a Mystery Shopper has grown in recent years as an indicator of quality. • This can be used to gauge the quality of a product or a service. • Typically a member of the public is trained to act as a 'normal' shopper, when in fact they are analysing and evaluating their shopping experience or the quality of the product. • The employees of the business are unaware that this is taking place, so very important and accurate feedback can be received about the customer experience.		